POPULAR MYTHS DEBUNKED

LAKSHMISHA THANTHRI

BLUEROSE PUBLISHERS
India | U.K.

For permissions requests or inquiries regarding this publication, please contact:

BLUEROSE PUBLISHERS
www.BlueRoseONE.com
info@bluerosepublishers.com
+91 8882 898 898
+4407342408967

ISBN: 978-93-5989-273-3

Cover design: Sadhna Kumari
Typesetting: Pooja Sharma

First Edition: March 2024

Dear Readers,

This is Lakshmisha Thanthri. It was my wish to write a very useful book from a long time. Corona virus break time gave me an opportunity to write one.

I have chosen few topics from several ones which have pricked my mind over last 15 years. I have put words to my thinking about those topics and expressed my views on those few chosen topics.

Aptly, called "Popular Myths Debunked". This 33-page handy book will surely provide a perspective which you would have not thought through.

On Few topics, readers may not agree immediately since they are heavy to assimilate quickly, and on very few topics, readers may not agree even after long time and its fine as we can always agree to disagree.

I have referred for data accuracy and information sourced from highly scared and rare write-ups from Indic scholars and historians read over a period of time. They are not found if we google and googling for all information accuracy can be misleading. However, on many occasions, even information is found on googling and analysing the said information to get meaningful insights for accuracy.

Myths are highly perspective based and exposing them through break down and by information analysis has been done. Still, there can be different views and its perfectly fine with me as my intention is to place my honest views on these topics and even if few myths are busted, then my job is done. At least, the book will open many people's thinking cap.

Happy reading and if you like it, kindly refer others whom you think should read this book.

[Lakshmisha Thanthri]

Bengaluru.

Lakshmisha.thantri@gmail.com

Below are the Chosen Myth Busting Topics

1.

Indian Democracy Copied from British.

In my younger days, I was told that the Britishers gave us democracy as a result of freedom struggle and the entire democratic set up is modelled after British system.

Well, let us trace the origin or first recorded instances of democratic rule in the world. No, it's not in France or in Britain but going several centuries and millennia back in then bharath.

There are recorded instances where Voting was conducted to elect representatives from among common people to lead and govern at village and taluka levels for better administration by the then rulers of bharath. This kind of system is still found in panchayat level in villages of modern India and also the Judiciary is managed by the village elders or representatives elected by voting.

Also, there were council of ministers for every king who were handpicked based on their knowledge prowess and capabilities. This is similar to present day setup where we have every minister govern different ministries based on domain. Also, we still have Rajya Sabha system where distinguished and accomplished people still get handpicked by various political parties.

Many large and flourishing kingdoms had several leaders either handpicked or by voting to take care of individual provinces and all these leaders rolled up to one ruler similar to present day system where MP's role up to PM.

Then flourishing Bharath's administrative, judiciary, accounting practices fascinated many foreign traders and visitors who carried it into their homelands. Thus, the influence of democratic set up from India was huge on Europe who adopted it into their region as per their requirements.

So, coming back to this century, when britishers left India, committee was formed under Leadership of Ambedkar to draft the constitution. Ambedkar's team took utmost care and drafted constitution as per Indian requirement without copying. If the constitution is read and understood, people will realize that its completely home-grown drafted by Indian talent. There could be minor influences from British rule, but Britain and Europe itself had adopted democratic system through Bharath influence.

Our judiciary still has traces of British influence, but our legislation is completely Indian and the constitution rules have been amended several times over a period of time by ruling parties making it even more local by nature.

Well, now it is clear that its completely wrong and false to say that democracy was a gift by Britain to India. Unfortunately, google searches and looking up to

Wikipedia doesn't give the correct picture on democracy, its rise and influences. Vested interests have propaganda about western dominance and maintainability and history is not recorded as it should have been.

2.

English is not Indian.

There is lot of resistance to English language in India.

Political Leaders view it as British hangover and should be used only for global purposes or in abroad visits.

It is true that local languages should be encouraged and used widely and there is no substitute for mother tongue. This is correct, but discriminating English is also not right.

Let's trace its origin.

It has been established beyond doubt that Sanskrit is the mother of all languages including English. Sanskrit

Travelled through ancient Indi Vedic people to Europe and middle east long back when the European civilization was still getting formed and was widely nomadic and in stone age era. Europeans got educated by literature work of Indic scholars on grammars, Vocabulary etc. and subsequently local flavours like English, German, Spanish, French grew. But, as research has established, Sanskrit was the root and mother of all these languages.

Even present-day English has many words which are derived from Sanskrit. If we do research on all the present-day English words, roots of those words trace to Latin, Greek, Roman, German, French, Islamic, Indic origin. If we further drill down on origins in Latin, Islamic, Roman, German, French, Greek words, they all point to Indic Sanskrit influence.

Also, Indian English has matured itself as a flavour just as French English or American English.

As globalized world, every region has taken on specific global responsibility which has been gifted by the way world has polarized over millennia. Ex, America has money and military prowess, Africa has environment and natural resource abundance and India has been the mother of all regions, Religions, civilizations and we call Vishwa guru as all roots and origins point to Indic or sanatan dharma of Vedic period of Bharath. In this way, Britain got the responsibility of global language prowess by means of English which got evolved by fusion of several language influences across globe whose roots all point to Sanskrit. Hence, Indians need not treat it as alien as it's a language gifted by their Vedic ancestors and has taken the present form which has an Indian English flavour be itself.

Yes, Hindi as national language should be encouraged and used as it is also a subsidiary of Sanskrit in its grammar, text etc. Hindi has evolved over a period of time through Sanskrit as common mass found it difficult to master Sanskrit language. It's a substitute for common masses of India for Sanskrit. Also, there cannot be substitute for local language and all regional local language should be used in daily communication and wherever interaction across states happen, then Hindi should be widely used.

Now, coming back to English, as the world is shrinking due to globalization, it is widely used and definitely a common Indian can use it freely may be up to 25 %. In this way, national and local languages are also in usage because it is through language that culture, traditions, society preserve and thrive.

More the language one learns and uses, it helps in brain IQ level. Most of the present day educated Indians usually speak, read up to 3 languages easily.

That is really commendable. Someday, Sanskrit will and should also get its due importance and many will and should use it since it's a god gifted language which helps a person's IQ level increase, better command over literature, communication etc. This has been proven by recent research on Sanskrit by Eminent researchers.

3.

IT software and hardware are foreign by origin.

There is a popular belief that IT was started by West and Indians learnt it and are serving them by their programming skills. This is not true.

Although Mainframes were created way back in early 19th century in America, the essence of programming was found in 18th century in present day Kashmir were Indian mathematicians developed musical instrument which produced sound based on algorithm. Our ancestral mathematical Vedic scholars had invented right from zero to Pi and to Fibonacci series. Even pyramid and palindrome mathematical formulas were

Produced by India. Prime numbers, binary series, sorting algorithms references are found in Vedic mathematics. So, maximum basis of present-day programming was already defined by our Vedic mathematicians. West used it to develop their technological system. In late 70's and early 90's when there were technological innovations started happening in west, there was similar development happening in India which was completely home-grown. The HCL Systems produced first mass Desktops which was completely indigenous. Several small firms in India created Assembly and machine programming in producing basic software's and hardware's. These became early Indian technological platforms which was completely home-grown. Similar developments happened in US and Europe as well at the same time.

The Indian talent started getting exported to US in late 80's. There is Indian innovation hand in creating Pentium chips by Intel which was widely used in PC's.

Again, there was an Indian hand in creating Sun microsystems which produced Java programming language which revolutionized programming and software development. It is the Indians who are contributing tremendously in open world software and tools development programmes. All major IT Companies in world have more than 30 % Indians on-board and some are heading the companies to newer heights. Ex Microsoft, google, oracle, IBM.

Even there was Indian hand in creating the Google search algorithm. The present-day Social media giant Facebook idea was originally from an Indian which was taken over by Zuckerberg. You can google to get the inside scoop. It was Bose work in early 19th century on sending messages wirelessly is the basis on which Instant messaging apps got developed. Again, the emails were an Indian creation by name sabir Bhatia which was bought over by Microsoft. Some of the best software's and hardware's that are running in the world are developed by Indians worldwide. Indian footprint in technological advancement in the world is very strong right from inception to next generation marvels like AI etc.

Let's take a step back and go back several millennia backwords. Our Sanathana dharma was bustling with technological innovations like flying objects, performing surgeries, mass destruction weapons etc. Technology was always in the forefront from time immemorial in ancient India, but lost somewhere in current millennia until 19th century, where again a technological revolution is taking place along with rest of world and Indian contribution is magnanimous in creating, expanding and serving the world.

Indians are again in driver seat in creating maximum start-ups as well as in next generation innovations in AI, Cloud computing, Analytics etc.

As long as we know that technology is there to help humans in their day to day activity and not to make us slaves of technology, we are fine. Discretion in using technology on need basis and maintaining a distance in not allowing it to take over human nature, that attitude and approach is good.

Hence, having aversions towards technology is not good either. Also, the criticism that technology is imported by west is an ill-founded propaganda and the truth is already explained above.

4.

BMI index – for healthy and perfect body.

BMI –Index is developed by nutritionists as the benchmark for perfect health and body by means of giving range for height and weight parameters.

BMI –Charts are referenced by doctors, nutritionists, health agents and most of time end up recommending tablets like calcium, iron etc and unwanted curtails on having full meal courses for normal people thereby propelling Pharma market and nothing else. This has taken scam proportionate worldwide and needs to be addressed. Also, unnecessarily a normal and above average looking guy are given that they are unhealthy thereby inducing unwanted complexes making them loose sleep as health and looks are paramount for most of people.

Firstly, Age is never considered in most of BMI Chart which is gross negligence. Age has influence over weight definitely. As people age, they do put on little additional weight especially in middle ages like 35 plus to 50 years range. This has to do with metabolism level. Then weight stabilises to a healthy range based on height, gender, race. We can easily say that the +10 Kg weight on top of the higher range in BMI weight chart is still normal for middle aged guys. +5 kg additional infact gives them the kind of body looks suitable with their personality making them look more perfect. Whoever has created the myth that even slight bulge with age is unhealthy needs to rethink on their understanding. As mentioned, for middle aged guys, a slight bulge with additional +5kg gives the more attractive physical attributes. Even, our ancient scholars, Vedic pandits, kings etc had this attribute which made them even more attractive since it gave them mature, learned, experienced and warrior kind of appearance.

Our cinemas are another bottleneck along with entertainment magazines which has propelled these kind of BMI benchmarks. Entertainment industry has only depicted that tall and 6-8 pack is what makes a perfect hero. People do get influenced by such depictions and notions. Infact, they have gone one step ahead and shown that clean shaved chest of men is perfect. This is rubbish as hairs around chest makes a man more masculine and attractive.

I want to re-iterate that both men and women especially middle aged to accept slight tummies as its perfectly normal with age. Infact acceptance indicates that a person is living in reality of age and the physical attributes would definitely match with the individual personality making them even more ripe and beautiful.

Anything above +10 kg on top of higher index of BMI Weight range is indeed a minor concern and needs to be looked at. That still doesn't mean that the person is unfit or unhealthy.

For being fit, a minor daily walk routine, or a yoga stretch or additional physical activity or association with a sport is all that is required for many normal people requirements.

I want to stress that there are people who are perfectly in sync with BMI index parameters and it takes a tremendous will power to maintain it. Criticizing them is like starting another myth which is not the purpose.

Kudos to them. Purpose of this topic is that to see normal people as normal even if they vary on BMI Index charts. They are also Healthy and beautiful.

Many Normal people are pushed to take up gyming since they vary on BMI Index chart and they don't require extensive workout sessions daily to feel and stay healthy. I have nothing against gyming as people who like it should take it up as gyming has many benefits like stress reduction, overcoming mental strains, toughness, fat reduction, lean body etc.

5.

Fairness means beautiful.

This write-up has nothing against being fair. Off course many gorgeous ladies and men are fair. This is against prejudice and colonial hangover that everything fair is the ultimate beauty.

Opposite attract. So is knowledgeable man and woman knowing that they are more attracted to skin colour different from theirs. I'm fair and was always attracted by weatish and brownish colour women. But knowing self leanage is more difficult than understanding other aspects. In the growing years, it was always back in mind that fair is beautiful and since we are fair, it is fair to expect fairer girls. But during marriage alliance time, most fair and good-looking girls did not compile to say yes and only when a weatish girl was proposed, consent came in. By digging self, self-realization about prejudices and attraction downed in.

If you look around, smart and very fair men and women get pulled towards dusky ones and viseversa.

Infact dark or black is beautiful. Many Europeans and oriental people are attracted towards darkish and brownish appearance. It's not an absolute rule that opposite colours attract and those who don't feel attracted are not smart. Then, that would create another prejudice.

Also, skin colour changes with time. Sometime becoming more lighter or brighter. For some Asians, skin melanin opens up during older days and they start having milky fairness. But unfortunately, dermatologists treat it as skin disease instead of treating it has natural evolution of skin tone. Few, spot double shades of colour and trust me, that is more beautiful than others because skin colour is not uniform, but diverse in them which has to be held with high esteem. Unfortunately, people attribute dual tones to some skin issue and discriminate.

All kind of cosmetic advertisements and people opinions drift commoners to believe that being fair is the best and ultimate gift.

A minor dark line on top of dusky or weatish colour people make them even more attractive. Again, its dual tone. Unfortunately, even Dermatologists will make you believe it's some kind of skin disease. There cannot be any substitute for natural appearance, but beauticians insist on putting make-up to look more fairer only. These are highly prejudice notions against other skin tone other than being fair.

Our ancestors held dusky, brawny and weatish colour people with high regard and they were right to some extent. Fairness was not treated as something special, it was just another skin tone. But, arrival of britishers changed the scenario.

It will be good if modern India learns something from our ancestors prior to British rule and give equal importance to all kind of body colour without discriminating. At the end, it's just a body colour, but there are more to physical appearance than just colour. And above, it's the individual personality that will ultimately attract and shine.

I will close this topic once again saying that I'm fair and some of the best and beautiful women in my surroundings are all fair. But other skin tone flavours are also equally beautiful and there should be no prejudices against them. To some extent, media, Movies and British Hangover are not being all inclusive in honouring diverse skin appearances.

6.

Science and religion are two separate streams.

It is often said that science and religion do not gel well.

It is believed in current intellectual circles that a very Religious person usually will have less regards to scientific values and more to superstitious beliefs.

This is absurd. Infact, if a scientist performs religious rituals, he is branded as bigot and scientists with atheist mindset are branded as rationale thinkers and considered superior. Again, a narrow-minded conclusion.

Let me explain. A very devout Hindu who is well echoed in his religious beliefs can have exemplary scientific temperament also. This was the case several centuries ago in ancient India.

All the great innovations in world have originated from India and all of them have the footprint of Vedic scholars and saints who were very devoted towards their religious practices. Infact, for a highly realized Hindu, science and religion co-exist and all religious practices are echoed with scientific reasoning. Our ancestors have created religious rituals and traditions in such a way that it has scientific effects and are carried forward for generations by common people

Through religious practices.

Usually a highly realized Hindu who is in pursuit of knowledge and moksha will show exemplary scientific

Curiosity and ends up discovering newer innovations in his chosen subjects. Religious practices are an extension of scientific values. They are interlinked and are not separate streams.

But, western thinkers have been systematically enforcing their views that science is different from religion and is true for Hindus as well.

This is not true, atleast for Hindus because Hinduism is a way of life echoed with reasoning. Let us remember that many great scientists were great saints too and a person is saintly through his religious indulgements.

Hence, for several millenniums, for Hindus, Science and religion co-existed and are not separate streams altogether. There is no strong justification why that should change now.

We should celebrate diverse ways of achieving scientific milestones (Religious, less religious, Non-religious etc.) by various globalized nationals rather than propagating one way.

7.

Hindu devas and stories influence multiple wives – male dominated.

It is a general notion among current rational thinkers that Hindu devas and associated life stories influence multiple wives and propagate male dominance. This is false.

There are crores of devas or gods in Hindu religion and if you do a count, female goddess outnumber male god count. It means, Hindus always worshipped women power as Devi or nari Shakthi. Even our rivers, land, resources are referred by feminine gender like matha,

Mathrubhumi, ganga, Saraswathi etc. Our ancestors knew that the source of human birth and sustainability is by women. They were protective about life giver and source. Even, in marriage rituals, men take dharmic oath that come what may, they will protect, take care and nourish their spouse. women were always given equal partnership. They were given education, consulted in governance and it was widely believed that if women power is suffering, the kingdom will suffer and is doomed. As men are physically masculine due to their biological makeup, they were warriors for most part of our history. Women were also warriors, but limited and were taking care of more important tasks of running household, businesses (dairy farming, agriculture, financial matters, children upbringing, social impacts, arts etc.). women were always equal in ancient India and their power was celebrated.

Now, let's look at our deva stories. Shiva married only once. i.e., Parvathi, although there is a story of first marriage to sati, who later Re-incarnates as Parvathi. It is more of remarriage. Our gods represent different Shakthi of nature. So, Shiva symbolised the power of withstanding personal losses and bringing back life to track. That was his personal story. Lord Vishnu was always with Lakshmi. But, he comes back as Srinivasa to Earth when Lakshmi had left him due to personal hurt. Then he falls for Padmavathi and it is Lakshmi who learns about it and comes back and get them married. In Hindu Marriage System, if all persons agree with heart, then 2 wives are possible. This situation does happen in unforeseen circumstances as in Lord Vishnu case. Even as per Hindu marriage act even today, this is permitted.

Usually, King sized Heartily personalities get attracted or have crush or affections and love to multiple females in their life journey before settling with love of their life. This theory holds good even today regardless whether a person is Indian, European or American etc.

When we look at other avatars like rama, he was married only once and infact set our dharma right by staying with one wife, i.e., goddess sita. Lord Krishna time was different. It was wartime in our history period and anywhere a country is occupied in wars, multiple marriages happen as an exception. This is to give some justice to all ladies. Lord Krishna was very practical and due to his time and situations, he did marry multiple times. That is an exception and exceptions has happened in history wherever the land is occupied by wars. Our other gods were mostly single, or married once like Buddha, Lord Brahma, great godly saints etc. so, our ancient history needs to be digged and understood as what they stood for before conclusion.

As explained, there is no other country where women or nari Shakthi are celebrated as in India. Our Devi avatars and stories are widely popular. Our history of devas does suggest to marry and stay with one. A proper insightful understanding is what is required.

8.

Indian large population – burden.

When I was in missionary school, our teachers often said that India is a rich country, but people are poor.

Large population has always been seen as a burden

By the corridor of power.

As I grew and went around the world, I realized our population or human capital is one of our primary strengths. West has abandon land resource, but people are less and are aging. In many countries like Germany, population growth is zero percent. It means no human capital for future unless you accept immigrants. How come such parameters are not used in arriving at economic and developed status by renowned economists. Also, another primary strength of Indian resource is that its largely peaceful with diverse backgrounds. It speaks about the maturity level of India as civilized. Maturity of civilization or human capital is not considered as key ingredient for any wellbeing of a nation. Another sore point for me with economists. The rich social norms, traditions, family values, culture, heritage and history are always important factors and all of them are not considered by any economists in determining "Developed" status.

The current Indian population is hugely young.

They are dynamic and full of talents. Yes, providing jobs is a challenge, but in this globalized world, Indian talent is always in great demand and even the rural crowd have opportunity due to sustained economic growth in past couple of decades. So, there are jobs and opportunity for the large crowd. This kind of human capital is not found anywhere except in China.

Instead of seeing it as a strength, we have been told repeatedly that it's a burden.

India is big enough and has enough land, natural, wealth resources at its disposal that everyone's needs can be met as long as people deserve and earn it.

Off course, having 5-6 children and above per family is not desirable for any country and there are pockets in India especially in rural and minority clusters where this kind of issue is still existing. Its matter of another decade, where even this will be controlled.

Having 2 children per family is healthy, sustained growth for future and good for society, family and already we see this happening among educated middle-class mass which is big in India. Even 3 children per family is growth and it should not be discouraged or looked down because we might reach China's state very soon very fertility rate among women is lowest because of 1 China policy. It is disaster and we don't want that kind of irreversible family production control mechanism

I get irritated every time I hear that India is poor and third world country etc. This is reflecting colonial mind-set as that is the expectation for them.

Infact, I have travelled to USA and every time I'm told that India is developing and USA, Europe are developed nations, I beg to differ. My request for economists is that please at least consider few of parameters that I have mentioned as development and sustainability indicators. You will realize that India is no less than any other nation, infact ahead in many aspects. Already seeing my great country reclaiming its Vishwa guru status and its large population which is young, dynamic and talented makes it happen. So, Large population has actually helped India and definitely not a burden.

To make my point even clear, go and talk to a remote villager in some deepest corner in India and strike a conversation. You will realize their maturity, hardwork, knowledge, family and social values. That is the real power of India that I'm talking.

9.

Arranged marriage – marrying someone without love is regressive.

Nowadays, we see a propaganda by the entertainment industry that without love and knowing the other half, how can you marry? They have Romanticised love stories so much that young men and women in India question the arranged marriage system and find it regressive.

Arranged marriage is a system pretty deep rooted in India from time immemorial. Also, love marriages are also happening from time immemorial. They are 2 different faces of the same coin and ultimately, the couple will be married and in love. But, criticizing one system for no fault is not right.

Arranged marriage is somewhere linked with the caste system which provides a kind of social security for communities.

Elders arrange the potential proposal. They would have looked at compatibilities like upbringings, economic equations, education, traditions, family and social values, physical attributes, occupation equations etc.

Only when the boy and girl also give consent, then the engagements, marriage happens. When couple start living together, they bond, develop likings, affections and also understanding for the spouse and finally love blossoms. Then kids happen and finally a family is in place. Elders and parents play key role in this entire journey.

It can be easily said that in India, not only bride and bridegroom marry, families also marry. It is true to some extent. Our society and community get enriched.

Nowadays, people have become more open. They arrange multiple meetings before consent is given so that some ground understanding is in place. Also, communities have started arranging potential matches from societies outside their circle. This arrange marriage system has worked. If you look at statistics,

Failure in love marriages are more than in arranged marriage. Society acts as a level fielder and family and Social circles ensure minor issues do not snow ball into separation in arranged marriages. It does take time for understanding each other.

In love marriages, there are many instances where couple realize that compatibility is difficult and family compatibilities usually suffer. Root cause is that some crush, or affection or passion or attraction is misunderstood as love. Love is not something that happens instantly like in films. Love is a journey where each other becomes soul mates.

Earlier, there were lot of resistance in India for love marriage outside the community, but things are changing especially in middle class circles. But, love marriage is still a taboo in interiors of India which needs to change and it will change with time. caste and community bonds are deep rooted in rural parts. Caste is by occupation and not by birth. That is what our Vedas have told. But, rural India usually doesn't get it and love marriages are not encouraged.

Right from rama-sita, to Vishnu-Lakshmi to

Krishna-Rukmini, arranged marriages have been in place. At the same time, Krishna, Vishnu have love stories also. As I said, they are 2 different streams and one should not be put down for the sake of the other. In a multicultural, multireligious, multiregional country like India, love brings and bonds people from diverse background and has helped immensely and probably that is the reason our entertainment industry thinks Love marriage is the way. Also, they have backing from Western culture.

Anyway, arranged marriages are sacred and is a system in which our entire forefathers followed, my grandfather followed, father followed and I'm following and has been working. It clicks. But, no way, I'm against love marriage as it has its own course. As I said, love is a journey where couple become soulmates and may all reach that stage in whichever path chosen.

10.

Being spiritual means giving up materialism, Comfort, Luxury.

There is a general feeling among masses that a person on spiritual path does not require materialistic life, comforts, luxury.

Being spiritual does not require to relinquish anything except elevating the conscious to higher level through

Yogic practices. There is no need to leave family and go to Himalayas. That is not being spiritual but being vairagya or sanyasi who does not want anything, but wanders around seeking salvation. There is a clear distinction between being on spiritual path and being on sanyasa path.

This materialistic world requires many achievers who are deeply spiritual. Reaching to higher state of mind through yoga is also an achievement and it can gel well and co-exist in an ambitious and go getter personality.

When a person achieves huge success by means of his work and talent, as a by-product and tribute, life would have rewarded enough riches like cash, land, gold, vehicles, luxury items etc. The same person can also be spiritual where his mind has reached higher state through yoga. He will be very clear on how to treat a material acquisition as a material.

He can enjoy the luxury that life has granted which he achieved. But as long he understands the detachments and limitations of materialistic acquisitions, it should be fine. Attachment on materialistic pleasures brings in selfishness and a spiritual person cannot afford that since pure happiness is in being in rightful path and enjoying the journey. Usually, a person on spiritual path will elevate his consciousness. In doing so, he would have cleared baggages, worldly attachments, bad gunas. He will be a pure gold in his soul, mind. That is the purpose of being spiritual so that one can enjoy life fully. People on spiritual path will be aware that they will accept materialistic pleasure by not wrong or unwanted means but by discharging their duties and talents and definitely their happiness in not dependent on acquisitions, but in the journey. Definitely one should not mind rewards and gifts that come in their journey by means of their work.

When big time achievers are also spiritual, it sets the tone and path for others to also follow because the world embraces and get inspired by successful people.

It means less misery and sufferings in the surroundings and that's why we require more and more spiritual seekers.

Definitely spiritual path and go getter paths co-exist and the world needs that deadly combination more than anything else.

END.

Thank You,

Lakshmisha Thanthri